CW00431143

This book is dedicated to all the wonderful families who follow my work, especially those who allowed me to share their stories and to my ever supportive family Stuart, Emily, Alex, Alana and Tilly for giving me the time and space to do my work.

DITCH THE DUMMY

The gentle way

CHANGE IS HARDEST AT THE BEGINNING, MESSIEST IN THE MIDDLE AND BEST AT THE END.

ROBIN S SHARMA

TABLE OF CONTENTS

DITCH THE DUMMY IN 5 DAYS

A NOTE FROM THE AUTHOR

WELCOME, AND THANK YOU FOR BEING HERE!

I am a speech and language therapist and mum of four children. I have worked with young children with speech and language delay and eating and drinking difficulties for the last 20 years.

I would often visit families at their home and strongly advise ditching the dummy, give a hurried explanation as to why it was important. I would then often sit back in my car and think 'it was easy of you to sit there and tell them to do that!" But for them to do it is going to be much harder.

Often parents would find it really difficult and I wasn't able to give them any time to support them.

I worked on a special care baby unit for a while and often advised using dummies as they helped neonatal babies tremendously to stay calm, provide pain relief and move them off tube feeding.

I would then be advising the same families a couple of years later to Ditch the Dummy.

When I left my NHS role to work for myself last year, the families that were finding me were often at the stage of ditching the dummy and so I set up a challenge on Facebook to help them.

The challenge quickly got media attention and it was featured in newspaper, radio and BBC The One Show. Parents were being sent my way and within a couple of months nearly 1000 people had taken the challenge.

I realised how helpful it was for parents to receive the relevant and correct information and to gain the support they needed to ditch the dummy. I got amazing feedback and so I have decided to write a book to support as many other families in the same way.

I can now refer all the families I support online to follow my easy gentle steps to ditching the dummy and hopefully take a giant leap forward to helping their child's development.

I hope you find it useful and look forward to hearing how you get on.

Joanne x

Joanne Jones
Consultant Speech and Language Therapist

PEOPLE WHO
SAY THEY SLEEP
LIKE A BABY
USUALLY DON'T
HAVE ONE

LEO BURKE

INTRODUCTION

workbook

INTRODUCTION

THE GENTLE WAY TO DITCH THE DUMMY

INTRODUCTION

I want to start this book with a huge welcome.

Thank you so much, I am so glad you have found me and my '5 Steps to Ditching the Dummy'.

The fact that you picked it up at all and have begun reading tells me you are a parent or guardian of a child who loves their dummy and that you are ready to ditch that dummy and move on to a dummy free life!

I once heard the phrase "when the student is ready the teacher appears' ... well here I am. I hope you get everything you need from this book.

I want to start by saying you are the expert for your child. You know what is best for your child, your family at this time.

My job is to tell you the facts, the ideas and the suggestions. Your job is to take it all in and then make the best decisions for your child.

This book is simple, it takes you through the steps hundreds of parents have been through to ditch their child's dummy in 5 days.

When I started teaching people my method to ditching the dummy I was unsure how it would work. I had spent years working with families to help their children and as a busy mum of four I knew that for me to follow things they needed to be actionable, simple and fast.

I started teaching my methods as part of an online challenge on Facebook and quickly saw lots of families having huge success and emerging dummy-free and super happy on the other side.

It is important to only start the ditching process when you are totally ready to do so as it is unfair on your child to start and stop. They will be confused and next time you try will be even harder.

Many of the families I worked with commented at the end 'It was so much easier than I thought' I really hope this is true for you too.

See you on the other side and if you need further help come over and find me. website details below x

HOW DOES IT WORK?

workbook

HOW DOES IT WORK?

THE GENTLE WAY TO DITCH THE DUMMY

WHAT TO EXPECT

So as you work your way through the book you will gain the knowledge, skills and confidence you need to ditch your child's dummy. You will pick up hints and tips and ideas as well as read stories of other parents who took this exact challenge.

Step 1 will talk you through all the reasons it is a good idea to ditch the dummy after the age of 1. I will talk you through 10 areas that are affected by dummy use, some you may have heard of before and others may surprise you.

In Step 2 I will help you to make a plan. Failing to plan is planning to fail and so I encourage all of my ditchers to make a plan before starting this journey. It take about 5 days to fully ditch the dummy. This is the average so don't worry if your child is slower or faster than this. I would encourage you to take some time to plan those 5 days; make them different and special in positive ways rather than focussing on the obstacle of ditching the dummy.

Step 3 is all about emotions and communication as well as getting into the right frame of mind to ditch the dummy. The key is that how you approach this emotionally is about 80% of the battle so in step 3 we get prepared for this.

In Step 4 we talk about emotional tanks. This analogy has single handedly helped my parenting journey. Find out about this awesome ingredient and how to use it to your advantage to becoming a successful ditcher.

In Step 5 you are ready to go! This is the step where you press the button. You go for it and ditch the dummy. From here you will need 5 days to get to a point where you have waved the dummies goodbye and begin to see the benefits of life without a dummy.

Are you ready? It is simple and very doable but sometimes it might feel tough. Parents in my challenge sometimes tell me they feel as though they are being cruel, or causing their children unnecessary upset but after they have completed the challenge they are always amazed at how well their child did and how much happier and more settled their child is without the dummy.

Let's get this going. Hold tight and head on into to Step 1.

Here is a little reminder... you can do this, hundreds have felt like you do and managed to complete the challenge. Have an open mind and a positive attitude.

INSTRUCTIONS: Keep yourself accountable and fill in this checklist as you go!

- [ ] READ INTRODUCTION
- [ ] COMPLETE STEP 1
- [ ] COMPLETE STEP 2
- [ ] COMPLETE STEP 3
- [ ] COMPLETE STEP 4
- [ ] COMPLETE MY PLAN
- [ ] DISCUSS WITH FAMILY AND OTHER CARERS
- [ ] COLLECT ALL DUMMIES INTO ONE PLACE
- [ ] FILL EMOTIONAL TANKS
- [ ] CELEBRATE A DUMMY FREE LIFE!
- [ ] DITCH THE DUMMY

IF YOU CHANGE
THE WAY YOU
LOOK AT
THINGS,
THE THINGS
YOU LOOK AT
CHANGE

WAYNE DYER

STEP ONE

ONE

workbook

STEP 1

In this chapter I would like to talk to you about the reasons why we are even talking about you ditching the dummy.

I am going to start with the positive and valid reasons you probably gave your child a dummy in the first place under the age of 6 months. Then we will look at ways that a dummy becomes less helpful as your child gets older.

Preterm and new babies

When babies are first born, sucking is a very important reflex. It regulates the baby's breathing and heart rate, reduces pain and there is evidence that it can reduce the risk of Sudden Infant Death Syndrome (Cot Death).

Often young babies need to suck not just for feeding, but also for comfort. Parents become reliant on dummies to help their baby be happy and calm.

If not breastfeeding a dummy is often is needed to help babies who need to suck for comfort and not just for nutrition.

6 months +

As babies, grow their muscles in the babies jaw, lips, tongue and face begin to strengthen and develop in their ability to move, and so prolonged sucking is no longer helpful.

However by this stage babies are often dependent on their dummy and look for it as a source of comfort as well as a sleep aid. Parents too become dependent on it as a way to soothe babies and provide calm and quiet.

Often this is the stage that parents will say, 'they love their dummy' or they 'won't sleep without their dummy'. Negative aspects start to become obvious too though, so babies wake when their dummies fall out, causing parents lots of night waking to replace lost or fallen dummies.

No-one tells new parents that although the dummy is helpful for the first few months, after the age of 6 months the re is a shift and the negatives begin to out weigh the positives.

As babies turn to toddlers they still enjoy the soothing effects of sucking but this is often when the damage starts to happen with the dummy. After the age of one, the benefits definitely outweigh the positives.

THE 10 REASONS
To Ditch the Dummy

CALMS AND SOOTHES

When the older baby and toddler is soothed by the dummy their heart rates slow down, their breathing slows down and they are in a 'pre-sleep' state. This means they take in less of what is going on around

NO ROOM TO PRACTICE

When babbling begins, children self practise to strengthen their tongue and get use to their own voices. However when there is a dummy in the way this practising happens less and sometimes not at all.

HIGH-ARCHED PALATE

Our tongue at rest should lie high in our mouths, touch the roof of the mouth from tip to the back.

This correct position helps the palate to grow in the right shape. Low tongue = high arched palate

EAR INFECTIONS

The tongue is also likely to lie too far forward in the mouth. This affects how children swallow and without a full, complete swallow the little tubes that free their ears of fluid don't get cleared adequately

MOUTH BREATHING

When the tongue is low in the mouth, often children will mouth breathe with lips apart. This has negative effects on adenoids, tonsils, snoring, sleep apnea and much more. Nose breathing is vital to good health.

SPEECH AND LANGUAGE

If a child has prolonged or excessive dummy use, it can delay their language development and cause problems with speech sounds such as lisping and using the back of the tongue to make sounds.

TEETH

Teeth are effected in two ways. One because the palate is narrowed and so the teeth do not have as much room to grow and are over crowded, and two because the front teeth are shorter and pushed forward leaving a gap.

FUSSY EATING

In some cases, children's muscles do not develop along the typical lines and this can make them fussy eaters as they do not have the tongue and jaw strength to chew foods.

WORKSHEET 1

QUESTION #1: What have you learned from this chapter ?

QUESTION #2: What surprised you most about how a dummy can affect development?

QUESTION #3: Do you see any of the negative impacts mentioned in your own child?

KIRSTEN & AMELIA

True Story

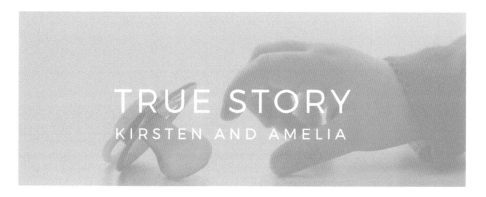

"AMELIA IS SO MUCH MORE TALKATIVE!"

Amelia was born at 34 weeks gestation and spent some time in the special care baby unit. The nurses there suggested a dummy to help Amelia as she suffered from reflux and found it difficult to settle. The dummy worked a treat and soon Amelia was sleeping through the night.

Kirsten, Amelia's mum planned to stop the dummy around 12 months of age but Amelia loved it. By three and a half Amelia was obsessed, she wanted it all the time. She would manage without her dummy at nursery but then ask for it as soon as Kirsten picked her up. Kirsten could see that Amelia's dummy was affecting her talking development but couldn't imagine Amelia being able to cope without it.

Kirsten saw the segment on BBC'S 'The One Show' and decided this was the time. She signed up there and then. Kirsten admits to feeling absolutely terrified at the start because Amelia would often have meltdowns when she didn't get her dummy.

The night before the challenge I told my daughter the fairies were coming to take her dummies for new babies. Kirsten was amazed when Amelia said 'okay' and they put the dummies in a little box by the fairy door. Kirsten recalls 'she did try to keep one saying, the fairies wouldn't want that one!', but soon agreed to give them all.

The dummy fairies were set to bring a special toy for Amelia as a thank you for the dummies. She chose a spiderman toy. Amelia had taken so long to agree to give the dummies up, that the shops were all shut. The next day I told Amelia the fairy had been stuck in traffic; a swift shopping trip and a few hours later, the fairy arrived taking the dummies and leaving a spiderman present.

Kirsten said "I think my partner would have given them back, but I cut all the tops off so he couldn't!"

Amelia was absolutely fine, a couple of times she said she missed them but these moments passed quickly. She is now so much more talkative!

I loved the challenge, it made me feel as though I wasn't alone and I got loads of support and advice. I never felt like I was a bad parent for having a dummy still at 3!

Kirsten finished by sending a message to other parents. 'It is nowhere near as bad as you think it will be or have built it up to be!

YOU KNOW YOU ARE A PARENT WHEN YOU HAVE CRAWLED UNDER A COT TO GET A DUMMY AT 2AM LIKE YOUR LIFE DEPENDED ON IT

ANON

STEP TWO
workbook

STEP TWO
MAKE A PLAN

SPEND SOME TIME PLANNING

What I found during the challenges is that the people who took time out to plan the 5 days had the easiest time.

"FAILING TO PLAN, IS PLANNING TO FAILURE'

Often we plough head first into new changes without taking time out to plan. When things don't work out we wonder why and what we should have done differently.

By taking time beforehand to plan things out, we dramatically increase the chances of things going well.

There are a few things I would like you to think about and plan for.

- **Read the whole book** - I would recommend reading the whole book before you start as this is going to help you to feel confident and put you in the right place to start, reading other people's real life stories will help you to see how this might work for you. I have deliberately kept this book short, easy to read and actionable so it doesn't become another thing on your to do list. get it read and then you are ready to start!!

- **Get support** - a good support system is a key factor. Join our Facebook group to chat to others who are going through the challenge at the same time as you. Post your questions and worries and comment on other people's to give them support.

- **The big collection** - are there a hundred dummies in your life? I have heard this so many times. In the car, toybox, squirrelled under beds... you name it! Before you start spend a few days collecting them. I have heard so often the story of the child finding a hidden dummy on day 4!

- **Your routine** - write down your routine and star the times your little one wants their dummy. Jot down some ideas of things you could do to minimise the need at this trigger e.g. avoid the television for a few days or the pram. Plan later bedtimes, an extra walk or naptimes in the car.

- **Comforters** - what comforts your child? A certain toy, extra cuddles, singing, music... whatever it is, have these things ready for when your child is upset. One of the things your child will be learning is new ways to self comfort other than suckling.

- **The whole family** - let everyone know the plan and get them on board. There are always situations where dad or grandma or nursery give the dummy because they didn't realise or didn't get the message. Start a Ditch the Dummy Whatsapp group!

- **Best distractions** - jot down your child's best distractions; for example, going outside, a certain toy or looking for dogs/cars/cats out the window. Have these up your sleeve for those moments your child is asking for the dummy.

- **Prize** - Is your child old enough to understand there will be a prize at the end? If so choose something that is motivating enough for them to work towards it. This really helped my daughter stop sucking her thumb. She wanted the prize so badly, it made her super determined.

- **Keep busy** - plan a busier than normal few days, do lots of things your little one loves and somethings you love too! Keep active and busy and avoid those dummy situations.

- **Bedtime** - if you haven't got a bedtime routine this is a good time to start one. Include a bath, a story and lots of cuddles. This will help your child to wind down without the need for sucking. If you already have a routine, look at mixing it up a bit. Maybe in the first week consider later bedtimes, more cuddles, special treats in order to help your child get comfortable with falling asleep without sucking.

- **In the night** - some children wake in the night the first few nights. So take so time to think how you will handle this. Don't do the challenge if there is a very good reason to need sleep. Equally, don't use this as an excuse as many parents comment it was not as bad as they feared. If the night waking is your only reason to put it off then I would suggest just go for it as it won't be as bad as you thought! I would also say often children's sleep improves once they have ditched the dummy!

WORKSHEET 2

INSTRUCTIONS: Jot down your routine and star all the times your child may want their dummy. Then write some ideas to get through those times e.g. go to the park, play lego, etc.

WORKSHEET 3

PLANNING DISTRACTIONS

INSTRUCTIONS: Spend some time jotting down times your child looks for comforters and distractions that will help your child during those tricky times. For example when they fall, watching TV

COMFORTER: DISTRACTION:

COMFORTER: DISTRACTION:

COMFORTER: DISTRACTION:

COMFORTER: DISTRACTION:

WORKSHEET 4

INSTRUCTIONS: Use this worksheet to plan out a bedtime routine for your child. Remember to think about how your other children will fit into it.

Start

JESSICA & OLI

True Story

TRUE STORY

JESSICA AND OLI

"Now Oli self comforts better than before."

Jessica gave Oli a dummy as a new baby as she wanted something that would help him to settle, but planned to get rid of it by the time he was 6-12 months.

Jessica found the Ditch the Dummy challenge in her local paper and was keen to have a go, as she really wanted to ditch Oli's dummy before his second birthday.

"My motivation" Jessica told me "was to stop the dummy to help Oli to start talking more. His dummy was always in his mouth 24/7".

Jessica was very worried to start the challenge as she couldn't imagine how it would go and wasn't feeling very optimistic about it working.

The day of the challenge Jessica asked Oli for his dummy and never gave it back. She was amazed at how well he coped and that night he only cried for 5 minutes before falling asleep.

From that day on Oli has never asked for his dummy or cried for it. On the Friday Jessica took Oli to the shop and bought him a present as a reward.

Before ditching the dummy Oli only had 10 words. Nine weeks later he has 45+ words and is using sentences.

Nine weeks later Jessica had forgotten where she had hidden the dummies, Oli asked her for a bathroom box and when he opened it, there were all the dummies. Jessica couldn't believe it! But Oli amazed her and said "ewww" and passed back the box!

Jessica said 'I loved the online group as I got so much support and everyone was so friendly and no one was judgemental."

Jessica's message to other parents is "Tell yourself you can do it. Your child will amaze you in how well they will accept the change."

A SLEEPING CHILD IS THE NEW HAPPY HOUR IN THIS HOUSE

JOANNE JONES

STEP THREE

workbook

TAKE TIME TO CONSIDER HOW YOU FEEL

This step is all about thinking about your emotions and feelings. If you are feeling scared and anxious and expecting your child to be angry, sad or traumatised, this is exactly what you will get. If you feel resilient, excited and positive, your child will pick up on this and they will cope much better.

"THE ENERGY YOU BRING TO THE CHALLENGE IS THE ENERGY YOUR CHILD WILL HAVE"

Getting rid of your child's dummy is not as simple as throwing an old object in the bin. It is much more complex than that and wrapped in some pretty complex emotions.

How you feel about the dummy will have a lot to do with your upbringing, your family's beliefs about dummies and the reasons you gave your child the dummy in the first place.

The dummy might signify to you an hours peace in the afternoon, or the ability to do your shopping in peace. It may even bring back warm fuzzy feelings from your own experience of having a dummy.

You may look at your child and see the safety, stability and comfort it brings and this may invoke feelings of guilt and unfairness at the thought of taking it away. Maybe you remember your own dummy being taken away and how you felt as a child in that situations.

The whole idea of change may fill you with dread, or the reality of your baby moving to the next stage fills you with sadness

These emotions may be the reason why you haven't yet ditched the dummy and may feel as though they are big, scary and looming worries.

I have some great news, thoughts and feelings are only that. Thoughts and feelings, they are not reality and can be changed in an instant.

STEP THREE
SORT OUT YOUR VIBE

I don't want that to sound too flippant or condescending and I definitely don't want you to think I don't 'get' what you are feeling. I totally do! I just know that with a bit of work you can change these feelings.

Thoughts lead to feelings, lead to words lead to actions.

In other words if you are, for example, worried about your child not sleeping without the dummy, this may then cause feelings of anxiety and worry. You will then let these emotions seep out in comments and words you say to your child or to others, You then focus your attention on looking for and reinforce your child behaving in a way that proves you right. This is human nature and we do this all the time. We look for evidence to support our beliefs to reassure ourselves that what we believe is right.

The voices in our heads are tricky customers and they are constant and pester for our attention. When you become aware of the fact that these voices are speaking your beliefs and a belief is a thought you think over and over again, You realise you can change your beliefs by choosing to think other thoughts.

If you focus on the positives of this process such as your child's talking more, sleeping better, having better teeth, this will in turn make you feel excited, happy and positive. You will talk about these expected outcomes and look for evidence to support it, this reinforcing the positive feelings.

So how do we flip this around. The first thing to do, is to allow your thoughts and feelings to come forward, listen to them, acknowledge them and work out why they are there. When we ignore them, they shout louder and more persistently so let them come up to the surface.

Grab a cup of tea (or glass of wine) and let all your feelings towards the dummy, your child, their babyhood and your childhood come to the surface and start to write them down.

By writing things down we are able to take a step back, be more objective and see these patterns for what they are, nothing more than habits that can be changed.

You can then begin to find more upbeat and positive thoughts to replace the emotionally charged thoughts.

I have provided you with some worksheets to work through this process.

Complete worksheet 5, leave it for a few hours and come back to it before completing the other worksheets.

WORKSHEET 5

REFRAMING

INSTRUCTIONS: In the left hand column I would like you to write down the thoughts and feelings you have about the dummy, how it helps you, how you feel, how your child makes you feel. Let your pen flow and write down anything that comes to mind. Wait over night and then fill in the right hand column with a different thought pattern that looks at the positives.

OLD STORY   NEW STORY

WORKSHEET 6

PINCH POINT - SOLUTIONS

INSTRUCTIONS: Think about pinch points in the day that are going to be tricky and where your child may struggle or you may struggle e.g. making dinner as my child will whinge and then think of a solution e.g. a week of easy preprepared dinners so I don't need to cook.

PINCH POINT: SOLUTION:

PINCH POINT: SOLUTION:

PINCH POINT: SOLUTION:

PINCH POINT: SOLUTION::

WORKSHEET 7

INSTRUCTIONS: Use this during this worksheet to jot down any emotions that come up for you. Writing things down really does help. Give it a go.

CIRCLE OF
EMOTIONS

VICTORIA

&

TODD-OLIVER

True Story

TRUE STORY
VICTORIA & TODD OLIVER

I COULDN'T HAVE DONE THIS WITHOUT THE SUPPORT

Victoria was terrified at the beginning of this challenge. She was worried she would never be able to help Todd to stop needing his dummy.

She took time to listen to all the advice and suggestions during the challenge and this gave her the confidence to believe that she and Todd were more than capable of ditching the dummy.

Todd had had a dummy from being a new born, but when Victoria saw the challenge on line she knew it was time to move on.

She asked Todd-Oliver to put his dummies on the cabinet and the dummy fairy would come and take the dummies and leave him some money. The next morning Todd was beyond excited and as soon as he opened his eyes he ran to the cabinet to collect his pennies.

There were a couple of moments after the first night that Victoria thought she may quit, but she held strong, telling herself to give it more time.

Jessica said 'Now, it's like he never had a dummy at all, it is like he has totally forgotten about it.

One of the main benefits for Todd-Oliver is that his speech sounds have improved and he is now pronouncing words much clearer.

Victoria highly recommends the challenge as she was amazed how little time it took. She says 'I honestly couldn't have done it without the ditch the dummy'

One thing Victoria wants parents to note is that Todd-Oliver went through a stage of pinching after the dummy had gone, but she felt this was a normal part of the transition and said it only lasted a very short time, so if this was to happen to you, then don't worry.

YOUR CHILDREN WILL BECOME WHO YOU ARE SO BE WHO YOU WANT THEM TO BE

ANON

STEP FOUR

FOUR

workbook

STEP FOUR
LOVE THEM THROUGH THIS

LET'S FILL THEIR EMOTIONAL TANK

We have talked about the importance of your mindset and how your vibe will affect their mood and approach to this transition. Well now I want to talk about *their* emotions.

Your child lives in the present, they are not thinking about how their teeth could be affected or how they need to talk more. They think tired = dummy or 'dummy dummy dummy!!!'

What is so important here is to think about this through their eyes. You must imagine how it would be to be reliant on the dummy for sleep, comfort, emotional regulation. When you do this and keep doing this you can't be cross with them when they whinge, won't sleep or cry. Children have big feelings and during this it could include confusion, instability and insecurity.

The great thing is you can reverse all these feelings for them in other ways. You can teach them other ways to self soothe, relax and sleep.

Children need us to love them hard and sometimes they will go to any level to get more and more and more of this love. You see, in the early days they learned that attention = love. So they crave more and more attention from you and others they love, in order to feel loved and secure.

For this transition period I want you to give them as much attention and love as you possibly can. I want you to fill their emotional tank until it is overflowing.

Have you heard of emotional tanks before?

This is an analogy for our internal emotional regulation system. It works like this. We all have an emotional tank and when it is filled with love (water), we feel amazing, calm, happy, content, loved and balanced. The problem is we get holes in our tank from things like lack of sleep, bad experiences, being shouted at, criticised or laughed at, the negative voices in our heads and the disapproval of those around us.

As the water leaks out of our tank we start to feel unhappy, frustrated, sad, overwhelmed or fearful.

We need our emotional tanks topped up and when we are little, we need others to do this for us, with attention, appreciation, praise, laughter, playing, kissing, hugging, being close, kind words, listening ear and being made to feel special.

STEP FOUR
LOVE THEM THROUGH THIS

The lower a child's level in their emotional tank goes the more extreme their signals that they need filling up are.

It doesn't make sense to us as adults that children who are being 'naughty' are looking for love.

Our brains go to a place that wants to show them the 'right way' to behave, to get them back 'in control' and 'show them who is boss'

By showing them the love they are craving, it feels as though we are 'giving in', 'letting them get away with it' or 'taking advantage' So our response is discipline and anger. This just creates more holes and the cycle continues.

If your child uses the dummy to plug some of the holes or provide a refill and we take that dummy away we need to be there with a whole lot of love to replace it and keep filling them quicker with more love to compensate for the holes.

The parents in my challenges that really embrace this concept have the easiest time, their children are the calmest and happiest.

This concept is often a new one for the parents I work with and they had never considered before that their child's behaviour was a cry for more filling of their emotional tank, but the visualisation helped many people to start filling rather than making more holes.

I always suggest to approach this transition as a team. Let your child know you are on their side, you wish you could make it better and you understand why they are upset. This type of language works so well. It can be tricky if no-one has used this with you before but give it a go and see how it makes you both feel.

This week could be one of the most loving and forefilling parenting weeks you have had so far and move you and your child into a closer and stronger place.

Don't forget you have an emotional tank too and as we get older there is more things and more people to make more holes! But the good thing is, as an adult you can refill your own emotional tank and you don't have to be reliant on others to do it for you. Spending time do more of the things you love, will help fill your tank. Doing things we enjoy such as playing sport, a hot bath, we may ask a friend for reassurance or read a book that motivates us.

Children need their tank filled by others and will learn techniques to get the refill they need such as whinging, crying, arguing, doing things that get attention, making others laugh, instigating play, sucking a dummy or sometimes withdrawing.

It is our job as adults to show children the best ways to fill their emotional tank.

So you can see that during a time like this, when moving away from the dummy the holes in your child's emotional tank will be more in number and bigger in size.

So we need to double our refilling efforts to help your child feel happy and safe.

It is easy to feel frustrated and turn to strategies such as bribing, threatening, shouting, arguing, punishing or being less available emotionally because your tank is empty too. This will only make bigger holes and make the whole process take longer or be less successful.

It is important to double up on filling that emotional tank.

Take a minute with the next worksheet (8) to think about ways your child enjoys being loved. It may be listening to you tell them something, it maybe rough and tumble play or being close to you or it may be reading them a book. Whatever they need, do it as much as you can over the next week or so.

In the following worksheet note down all the things your child does when they need an emotional tank top up.

What behaviours do they do to get attention (remember to them attention = love)

WORKSHEET 8

EMOTIONAL TANK FILLERS

INSTRUCTIONS: Use this space to write down all the things your child loves and things that fill their emotional tank. You could then stick it up on your fridge as a reminder when things get tough.

ABI&
MARTHA

True Story

"Replace the dummy with a rubber duck!"

Abi had a different reason for giving Martha a dummy in the early days. She suffered with postnatal depression and anxiety, and found it very difficult to cope with Martha's crying, particularly in public.

She always planned to ditch Martha's dummy by 12 months. When Abi saw the challenge on BBC 'The One Show' she was nervous and scared but decided to give it a go anyway. Martha's teeth and speech were beginning to be affected and so Abi was determined to make the change.

Abi really took onboard the need to plan for this challenge and she and her husband both made sure that she didn't have much work on that week and they planned their meals out beforehand. Tis ensured they had the time and energy to give Martha the extra time and attention they knew she would need.

They had already, without realising been implementing the stepping out and so when they started the challenge Martha was only having her dummy for naps and at night.

The first couple of days were hard and there were more tears than usual. It was hard to help Martha understand that her dummy was gone. She wasn't ready to understand the concept of the Dummy Fairy and so Abi just kept calmly repeating "dummy gone".

Abi decided to change up the bedtime routine a little and added in more stories and cuddles. The first couple of nights were tough, but then by the third night Martha had cracked it.

Even though it was tough at times Abi never felt like she was going to quit, she was determined and stayed positive.

Martha soon found a replacement for her dummy; a rubber duck! Now the rubber duck gets to sleep cuddled up in bed with her!

Abi says Martha is now much calmer and the amazing bit is that Abi can cope much better with her crying and has found other ways to deal with it.

Abi advises other parents to get organised so you have extra time to give lots of praise and cuddles.

I AM YOUR PARENT; YOU ARE MY CHILD. I AM YOUR QUIET PLACE; YOU ARE MY WILD.

MARYANN CUSIMANO

STEP FIVE
workbook

LETS THINK ABOUT THE HOW

I hope by now you are feeling inspired and confident to take on this parenting task. Although it is not easy, it is short lived and the parents in my challenges are always amazed how much easier it is than they thought it would be. Once you have decided that you are going to help your child transition away from dummies, it is time to think about how to do that.

There are three approaches you can take

1. **Stepping Out** -

In this approach, you would jot down all the occasions your child has their dummy during the day and night. So for example
- to sleep
- to rest
- to recharge
- when watching television
- in the car, for comfort
- when hurt,
- when sad
- when crying.

You then look at these and decide which would be the easiest to start with.

Which you child could cope with best and you go for it. For example you might say I am not going to give him the dummy when he is hurt , I am going to teach him other ways to self comfort or provide the comfort in another way.

You stick with this for 4 to 7 days, and then add another occasion, so for example the next step might be, not for comfort or when watching TV. This gradually weans your child off the dummy.

2. **Sliding out**

In this approach you give the dummy to your child for a short period e.g. during story time and when falling asleep but then take it off them once asleep. Or you let them have it for a few seconds when they are settling down and then taking it away as soon as they are settled.

3. **Cold Turkey**

Sometimes this is the hardest, sometimes the easiest. This would be when you take the dummy away totally and don't go back.

How to go Cold Turkey

Depending on your child's age, developmental stage and personality there are different ways to go about this. For example a younger child won't understand the concept of the dummy fairy and there would be little point in using too much language to explain. Older children can be brought into the process, given choices and told stories including their favourite characters or people.

In the dummy challenges parents have used lots of ideas to ditch the dummy. The key to it is to always start with steps 1-4, with this preparation any of them can work well.

Very young children (under 18 months)
At this age it is probably best to just do it. No language, lots of cuddles, reassurance and filling their emotional tank

Younger children (under 2 and a half)
With younger children it is best to use very little talking and lots of reassurance, calm words and consistencies.

Things that work well are telling the child the dummy is 'gone', 'broken' or 'lost' When the child looks for or asks for the dummy utilise one of your back ups, distract them and then give lots of love and praise.

Older children (over two and a half)
You could try the following:

- Get a book about ditching the dummy
- Tell them a story about someone ditching the dummy
- Tell them about the dummy fairy
- Use a character and say they are coming to take the dummy.
- Use a sticker chart
- Swap the dummy for a present
- Send the dummy to the dummy tree (https://growingsmiles.co.uk/the-dummy-tree-is-the-place-to-b)
- Give the dummies to a baby
- Give their dummy to Father Christmas.

When thinking of a story, look at it through their world, what do they like, what motivates them, what would they understand. Remember to make it positive, for example there is a difference between saying, "Father Christmas says you have to leave the dummy for him on the tree or he won't leave any presents" and "If we leave the dummy for Father Christmas he will bring you an extra special present".

Be consistent

It is so important to be consistent. Choose a time when you can commit to following through on this. If you start and then give the dummy back, that can make things so much harder for both you and your little one.

Use consistent routines, consistent rewards and consistent words and your little one will feel secure, loved and capable.

Language to Use

In my challenge I suggest to people to use 'inclusive' words. This means use words that put you and your child on the 'same team'. For example 'we can do this' and 'I know how you feel' or 'we are finding it hard now but I know it can get easier'. Think about times you have done something difficult and the things that have helped you, the words that make you feel heard, loved and supported or maybe the words you would have liked to have heard. Adopt these for your child. try not to talk about your child, or the dummy ditching to others.

Rewards

Plan a reward system that is really relevant to your child. For example, make rewards high value, don't make your child wait too long for the reward and if you have said you will do it, make sure you do it, this way you can keep your child's motivation high.

The Dummy Tree

You can send your dummy over to Leigh at Growing Smiles and she will put it on her dummy tree and take good care of it. She will take a photo of it and send it to you for your child to see. https://growingsmiles.co.uk/the-dummy-tree-is-the-place-to-be/

Thumb Sucking.

Some children replace their dummy with thumb sucking. If that is the case check Thumbsies for a way to move on from thumb sucking.

https://thumbsie.co.uk/

WORKSHEET 9

HOW WILL YOU DITCH THE DUMMY?

INSTRUCTIONS: Which method will suit your child the best. In the circles below choose your path and write out your three step plan. For example, if you choose Stepping out Step 1 could be 'The Car', Step 2 'Nap Time' and Step 3 'Bedtime'

SLIDING OUT   STEPPING OUT   COLD TURKEY

STEP 1

STEP 2

STEP 3

WORKSHEET 10

REWARD CHART EXAMPLE

INSTRUCTIONS: You can use this with your child as a reward chart or go online and print a reward chart of your child's favourite character. Use stickers or a coloured pen to colour in each achieved box. Don't forget to specify a prize at the end!

Start

DAY 1

DAY 2

DAY 3

DAY 6

DAY 5

DAY 4

DAY 7

And your PRIZE is...

NATALIE&
DARCEY

True Story

"I planned sliding out but my husband misunderstood and went cold turkey!"

Darcey had a dummy in the first few weeks of life as she was constantly feeding and the dummy enabled her mum Natalie to get some rest.

But by the time Natalie saw the Ditch the Dummy on BBC's 'The One Show', she knew it was time to say goodbye to the dummy as Darcey was drooling much more than other children her age and needed a bib.

Natalie was apprehensive because Darcey was such an amazing sleeper and the thought of changing that was scary! However, she reassured herself that Darcey was old enough to understand and was at an age where she could be bribed!

Natalie briefed Darcey's dad on the plan and said they would gradually reduce the dummy time and eventually get the Dummy Fairy to come with a gift. But dad only heard the bit "we are getting rid of the dummy". That night, dad took the dummy away and Darcey went cold turkey!!

Natalie was mortified!! It was not her plan but she was amazed that within 5 minutes Darcey was asleep! Over the next few nights Darcey would ask for her dummy but be easily distracted and with a promise of a present at the end of the week, Darcey was happily settling herself to sleep.

Natalie says "I was shocked but so proud at how well she took to it, I am so glad now we just went for it".

The Dummy Fairy brought Darcey a Rapunzel dress. Little did mum know this would be the only thing Darcey would wear for the next few weeks!!

Natalie says that Darcey is no longer drooling and her language is booming even faster than before.

Natalie says she is so glad she did the challenge, she found the information so informative and supportive and she would urge other parents to just go for it!

THE GREATEST HAPPINESS IS FAMILY HAPPINESS

BJARNE REUTER

YOU ARE ALL SET TO

GO
GO
GO

EXTRA SECTION

Bonus

THE GENTLE SLEEP GUIDE

Sleep is LIFE when you are a parent!

One of the big things that often holds parents back when they are thinking about ditching the dummy is the fear about bed time and sleep.

Here is my **10 step** gentle guide to sleep:

1. **Never use bed as a punishment.** If you send you child to bed when they are naughty they will view their bed or bedroom as a negative place. We want bed to feel like the cosiest, safest place on earth.

2. **Make sure their bedroom is uncluttered, calm, cosy, and welcoming.** Have soft lighting, warm bedding and good ventilation.

3. **Establish a lovely bedtime routine** that isn't rushed, includes lots of 1:1 attention and emotional tank filling. I think this can be hard as a parent you are often tired at this point and want to rush it, but try not to

4. **Red lighting** is sleep inducing and soft music/white noise helps some children fall asleep.

5. **Children need to associate items and routines with sleep.** The dummy will have been a big part of this so look for alternatives that your child likes.

6. **The first night plan bedtime** to be a little later, maybe have an evening walk or a play outside beforehand.

7. **Think about** how this is your child's first night in a new 'normal' and they may need some help settling.

8. If your child needs **help, cuddle them**, lie with them, sing whatever it takes to help them settle.

9. Night two, do slightly less to help, for example if you cuddled them to sleep, have them lie in bed and you sit next to them and hold hands. The following night sit next to them the but don't touch, the third night sit by the door. So you are **gradually fading out of the picture**.

10 Often saying that you will **keep checking in on them is reassuring for your child,** to know there is someone close by.

This gentle approach will minimise tears and show your child how to self settle. Within 5 nights many children will be nodding off on their own. But you can adjust it for your own child. The key is to keep moving a little further back each time or you could get stuck and become a new important tool for your child to settle. You need to be the transition not the replacement!

Room quiet and cool	Needs someone touching to fall asleep	Bed cosy and familiar
Has another comforter	Soft lighting	Needs cuddling to sleep
Relaxing music	Warm drink	Uncluttered room
Needs someone near to fall asleep	Spends time playing in room	Falls asleep alone

KELLY PADDY

True Story

"Paddy is eating, sleeping and talking better than ever!"

Paddy is Kelly's youngest child and with 5 older siblings all using dummies, Kelly didn't hesitate to give Paddy a dummy too.

With no plans to ditch the dummy, Paddy was 3 years and 3 months when Kelly entered the challenge. Kelly decided to enter the challenge as Paddy was eating less and less and she was becoming concerned about the small amount he was eating.

Kelly couldn't think of one reason not to join the challenge and the thought of joining made her feel empowered and so she set about finding out more.

Kelly took very decisive action and whilst Paddy was at nursery, she collected all the dummies from around the house and cut off the teats. She knew things were going to be dramatic when he got home but she knew the time was right. Indeed Paddy was not happy but for the first time ever he ate all his dinner and was in bed asleep an hour later because he just didn't know what to do with himself or his mouth!

The next morning Paddy's big sister, Nancy, came trotting downstairs with a dummy in her mouth. When asked why she innocently answered, "I hid one for Paddy just in case he was upset!" Mum swiftly took the dummy, cut off the end and popped them in the bin. Ten minutes later when she was trying to shower, Paddy appears with the chopped off teat on his finger trying to suck it!!

Kelly has no regrets about the challenge and said there was not one moment she thought about quitting.

Paddy is now eating better than ever, he is sleeping for longer and deeper and his speech has dramatically improved.

Kelly loved the challenged and urged other parents to take part. She said the best bit was that it was gentle, it worked and there was no parent shaming!

YOUR CHILD WILL
NOT REMEMBER
YOU FOR THE
MATERIAL THINGS
YOU PROVIDED BUT
FOR THE FEELING
THAT YOU
CHERISHED THEM

RICHARD EVANS

EXTRA SECTION

Bonus

GUIDE TO
LANGUAGE
DEVELOPMENT

Some children just learn to talk others need to be taught

Children develop language slowly over the first 5 years of life (learning is lifelong but this is when the most learning happens).

Very briefly and broadly speaking, here is what to expect from your child:

1. Children in their first year use crying, facial expression and sounds to communicate.
2. Children start to say their first words between 10 months and 15 months.
3. By 18 months, children tend to have a vocabulary of 20+ words.
4. By 2 years, children start to link together two ideas/words.
5. By 3, children are talking in phrases of 3+ words.
6. By 4, children begin to use grammar, word order and can hold a conversation.

If your child is not meeting these guidelines there is a lot you can do to help them. Here are my top 5 tips : (If you are worried please have a Speech and Language Therapist assessment.

- **Say what your child can say or would say if they could** - rather than testing or asking your child to say things, just tell them what to say.

- **Think of your child as a computer.** Input the information and wait for the output. Don't try to drag language out of them by asking them to say things.

- **Imagine you are a sports commentator,** in one word more than your child speaks, say what is going on e.g. if your child says single words you say two. If your child says no words, you say single words.

- **Reduce the questions and directions you give.** It is sometimes necessary to ask your child to do things, but limit how often you ask questions or give directions in a day.

- **Never tell your child they are wrong,** just say it back to them clearly and carry on. They need to feel as though it is okay to keep trying.

RUTH &
EMILY

True Story

"I realised the fear of not having the dummy came from me."

Ruth gave Emily a dummy after being advised by the Health Visitor. Emily was struggling to latch on and the Health Visitor suggested that Emily would benefit from a dummy to help her with her sucking.

Ruth said she never really liked Emily having the dummy especially as she got older. When she was out and about she always got the feeling that people were judgmental about an older child having the dummy.

Ruth's partner saw the challenge on the television and suggested she find out more. Ruth says she tried to ditch the dummy in the past but her partner always ended up giving it back to Emily because he didn't want her to get upset.

Ruth went through all the information about why to give up the dummy and this made her feel more determined than ever. She decided there and then she was going to ditch the dummy no matter what happened next.

Ruth said that because she felt so prepared, she was ready to get going, she planned exactly how it was going to go and she couldn't wait to start.

So on the day, Ruth took all the dummies away in the morning. If Emily asked for it she changed the subject and distracted her.

Ruth said the first night was awful, but she just held and comforted Emily because she understood how Emily must be feeling and could deeply empathise. When Emily drifted off to sleep in Ruth's arms, Ruth knew they could do this. She snuck downstairs and threw all the dummies in the bin. That was it, there was no going back!

Emily had always been a great sleeper but for around a week she woke in the night. Ruth comforted her and the phase soon passed. Ruth says she had the confidence to then ditch the bottles and this too went really well.

Ruth said "I learned so much about me and Emily during the challenge. I learned we are both stubborn but that Emily is more resilient than I thought and actually the fear of not having the dummy came from me."

Ruth loved the community of the challenge and chatting with other mums who were having the same struggles and going through the same things. Having all the information meant she felt able to complete the challenge.

DON'T LET YOU FEAR OF WHAT COULD HAPPEN MAKE NOTHING HAPPEN

DOE ZANTAMATA

EXTRA SECTION
Bonus

GUIDE TO
EATING &
DRINKING

Eating and drinking skills shouldn't be overlooked

Eating and drinking, like talking, relies on the development of the lips, jaw and tongue.

Babies go through certain developmental milestones which takes them from sucking to biting, chewing and swallowing complex family foods.

In order for this to happen the child needs to strengthen their muscles and they dot his little and often with practise.

Most children are motivated to eat and drink and so naturally get to practise moving their tongue. This first happens around 6 months and this is when babbling starts. Their muscles get stronger and movements become more precise the more they practice and by 12 months they are biting, chewing and forming clearer words.

Some children develop eating slower. This is either due to a motor difficulty, a sensory difficulty or a bit of both.

Motor Difficulty - if a child's' mouth muscles are not developing at the right pace, it is due to three main causes.
- **Neurological** - some difficulties with the brain that means the muscles can't move.
- **Tongue Tie** - a piece of tight skin under the tongue anchoring it to the floor of the mouth.
- **Lack of use** - either due to dummy use or aversions/illnesses that stop the child eating normally or moving their tongue in increasingly mature ways.

Sensory Difficulty - Some children experience the feeling of touch, taste and temperature in their mouth either more or less acutely than other children. If they feel these sensations more acutely we call this Hypersensitive and if it is less acute, we call it Hypersensitive. This change in sensory information can mean the child has strong dislikes of certain textures, tastes or temperatures.

It is quite common for children to have a mix of both sensory and motor difficulties. For children who don't eat well, stopping dummy use can really help as it allows the tongue to go through the normal stages of development and therefore helps the child to manage different textures.

EXTRA
SECTION
Bonus

IF EVOLUTION REALLY WORKS HOW COME MOTHERS ONLY HAVE TWO HANDS

MILTON BERLE

GUIDE TO
THE ONLINE
SUPPORT

BONUS SECTION
THE ONLINE CHALLENGE

Need some extra support?

You may have heard me throughout this book talk about the **online challenge.**

If you feel you need **more support** the online challenge may be just what you need.

Hosted on Facebook this **challenge group** is a great place to get the support from other parents and myself. You would be welcome to join to chat to parents going through the same thing and also to ask me qyestions.

If your child has speech and language development difficulties, I work online to support parents who are **worried about these difficulties** and you can find out more at www.joannejones.co.uk

Thank you so much for taking the time **immersing yourself in this book.**

I hope you have **found it useful** and look forward to seeing you in our community and **hearing your story.**

Much love,

Jo

MOTHERHOOD IS ALWAYS AN ACT OF COURAGE

STACY SCHIFF

Printed in Great Britain
by Amazon